Galaxy Mapper

Galaxy Mapper

The Luminous Discoveries
of Astrophysicist Hélène Courtois

ALLIE SUMMERS

illustrated by **SIAN JAMES**

≡ mit Kids Press

HÉLÈNE's eyes widened through her binoculars, stretching their way closer to the moon.

What is beyond the moon? she wondered.

Hélène's maman and papa had given her the binoculars so she could get a closer look at soaring mountain birds. But, in the evenings, the moon was waiting for her.

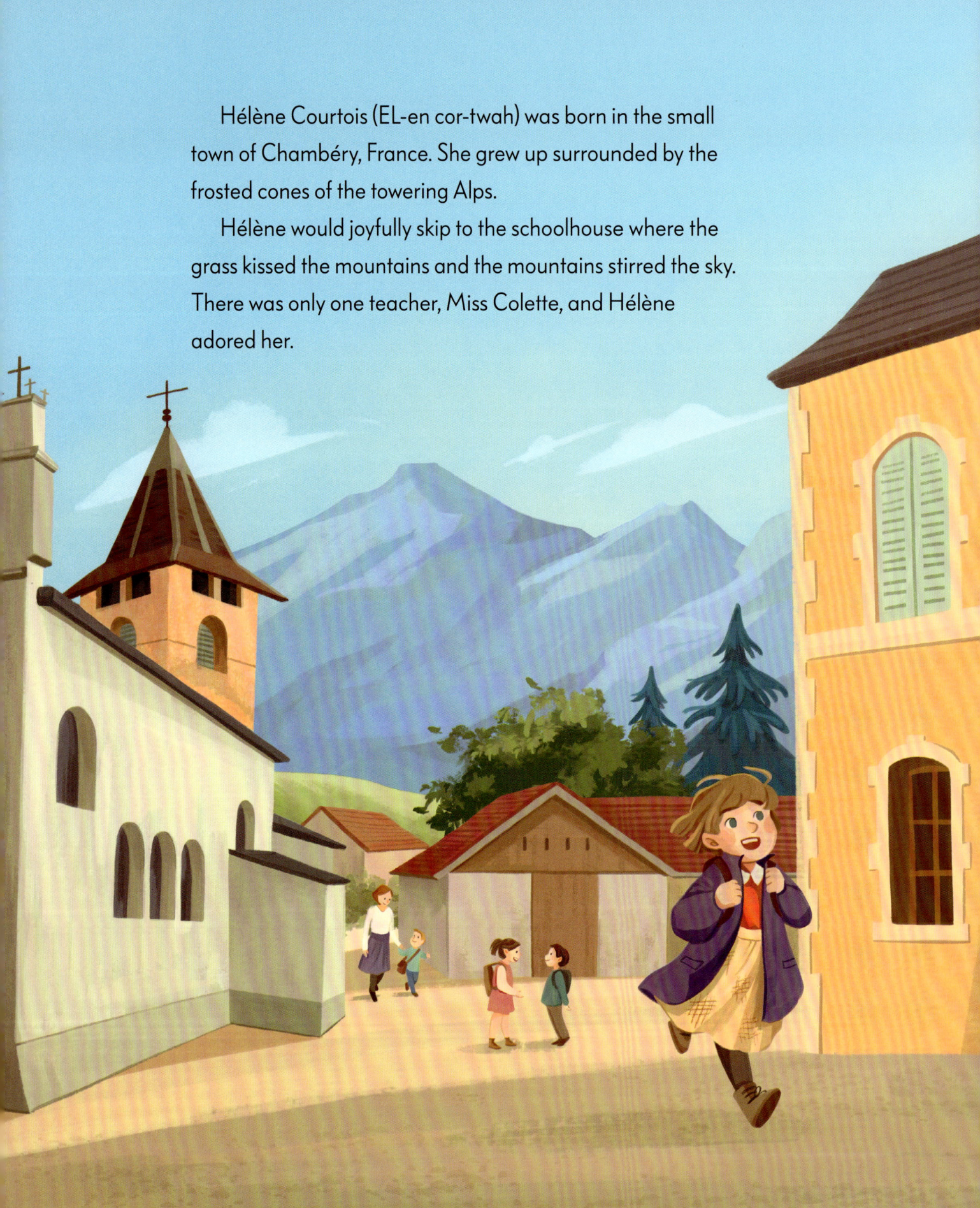

Hélène Courtois (EL-en cor-twah) was born in the small town of Chambéry, France. She grew up surrounded by the frosted cones of the towering Alps.

Hélène would joyfully skip to the schoolhouse where the grass kissed the mountains and the mountains stirred the sky. There was only one teacher, Miss Colette, and Hélène adored her.

Miss Colette would often take the class out into the forests and fields to explore. In the high grasses, Hélène watched caterpillars grow. *I wonder how much they need to eat before they get cozy and begin their transformation into butterflies?*

Hélène observed.

Hélène questioned.

Hélène had ideas.

And the moon was always waiting for her.

As Hélène got a little older, her parents taught her how to use a trail map to explore the mountains around their home.

"It shows the paths you can walk in nature, changes in elevation, and points of interest along the way," Maman told her.

"It's a mountain you can hold in your hand!" Hélène exclaimed with joy.

Out on the trails, Hélène watched snowmelt and rain find each other and flow down steep rocks, forming creeks, rivers, and waterfalls—finally gathering in lakes as clear as glass.

Sadly, all too soon, it was time to leave Miss Colette and the luminous schoolhouse. Hélène felt like she was being swept downriver to an unfamiliar place.

At her new school, she didn't like being in the classroom: sitting, listening, waiting.

As soon as the bell rang, Hélène was always the first one outside. She couldn't wait to gaze at the clouds swimming in the sky.

When Hélène was old enough to drive, Maman and Papa gave her a new kind of map: a road map.

"It shows you the routes you can drive, types of roads, and how they are connected," Papa told her.

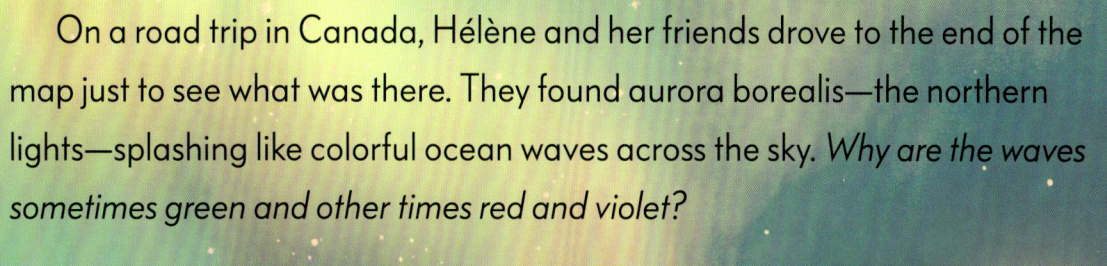

On a road trip in Canada, Hélène and her friends drove to the end of the map just to see what was there. They found aurora borealis—the northern lights—splashing like colorful ocean waves across the sky. *Why are the waves sometimes green and other times red and violet?*

Hélène observed.

Hélène questioned.

Hélène had ideas.

And, in the evenings, the moon was waiting for her.

Hélène decided to go to university to continue learning. But nobody in her family had ever been to university before. There was no map for this journey. Hélène arrived with the intention to study medicine, but a strong tide was pulling her away. It felt like the moon was nudging her to follow what she had been looking up at her entire childhood.

Within a few short months, Hélène changed her studies to **astrophysics:** the science of how planets, stars, and other natural objects in space begin, grow, and interact.

She glanced around her first class. *Where are all the girls?* she wondered. All her professors and most of her classmates were men.

Hélène remembered other fiercely intelligent female scientists who had made incredible discoveries within a school system full of men: Sandra Faber, Renée Kraan-Korteweg, Henrietta Swan Leavitt, and Vera Rubin.

They did it, and so will I!
Hélène told herself.

Although she mastered every formula and conquered every problem she was given, Hélène struggled to be heard. Just because she was a girl, some colleagues thought her ideas weren't serious. Once, she was even told she would never obtain a position as an astrophysicist!

She put their criticisms in an imaginary balloon and let it disappear into the night sky.

Hélène became sharply focused. *If I learn advanced **plasma physics**, I will be better prepared.*

Hélène observed.

Hélène questioned.

Hélène had ideas.

And the moon was always waiting for her.

On some nights, Hélène and her classmates could look at the night sky from the university's **observatory**. Gazing through the professional telescope, Hélène caught a glimpse of her first spiral **galaxy**.

She fell in love! Galaxies were the most beautiful things she had ever seen; she knew she could never take her eyes off them.

They were luminous lighthouses in the vast sea of **dark matter**. All over the sky, gravity had drawn in stars, dust, and gas and stirred them into swirling islands of glowing light.

Back in the classroom, Hélène was
introduced to her third type of map: maps of galaxies.

"Scientists can focus on mapping galaxies and other structures in
the **universe**," her professor explained to the class.

Hélène thought to herself, *If people who map land structures are called
cartographers, then people who map galaxy structures must be called* **cosmographers**.

Hélène's path became illuminated. She knew she would become a cosmographer
and map space landscapes that had never been seen before.

She set out on her first mapping voyage: to observe and analyze the **Great Attractor**, an area of the universe that appears to be pulling many galaxies toward it—like a fisher reeling in a galactic catch. It hides from our own Milky Way galaxy behind clouds of stars and dust, which makes it hard to observe from Earth.

Hélène had to travel to a telescope in Australia to see the section of the sky where the Great Attractor hides. During the days, she photographed emus and kangaroos and felt like a true explorer. Hélène marveled at how different the dry plains and volcanic spires of Australia were from the majestic Alps in France.

Like the native Australian boobook owl, Hélène's eyes stayed wide open at night: awake, alert, and searching the expansive sea of swirling stars. The galaxies she looked at were so far away that it took their light a very long time to reach Earth. In fact, the light that reached her eyes through the telescope took so long to get there that it had first started traveling at a time when dinosaurs walked on planet Earth.

Hélène captured lots of galaxy images with the Australian telescope and studied them with her team. She used a complex formula to figure out the distance, speed, and movement of each galaxy. Then Hélène added this information to a **dynamic map** that showed where the galaxy is located in the universe *and* how it is moving.

Hélène did this over and over again. Numbers swam with the stars in her brain. After all her complicated work, her map was not accurate enough. The formula she had used to position the galaxies created map lines that were too blurry.

For a moment, Hélène felt stuck, like a boulder in a river. But, quickly, she became like the water flowing around the boulder—and found a new path. *If I use the **luminosity method** to examine the galaxies, my map should be more exact.*

Hélène observed.

Hélène questioned.

Hélène had ideas.

And, in the evenings, the moon was waiting for her.

$$v_{CR}(r) = \tilde{v}(r) + \langle v(r)u_i^o \rangle \langle u_i^o$$

$$R_{ij} = \langle u_i u_j$$

$$\rangle = (\sigma_i^2 + \sigma_*^2)\delta_{ij}$$

$$\langle v(r)u_i^o \rangle \langle u_i^o u_j^o \rangle^{-1} u_j^o$$

At the end of the project, Hélène had mapped the location and movement of more than a thousand galaxies. This time, her map was accurate. It also seemed to confirm that the galaxies were moving toward something. *It must be the Great Attractor.*

She wished telescopes could get a little stronger so she could get a better glimpse of what was happening around the Great Attractor.

Hélène graduated from university and started working as an astrophysics professor. While Hélène taught and continued to research galaxies, telescopes *did* get bigger and stronger!

Almost ten years later, the strong tide tugged her back to her mapping quest. Hélène knew there was more to the Great Attractor, and she was going to map it. She assembled an international team to help.

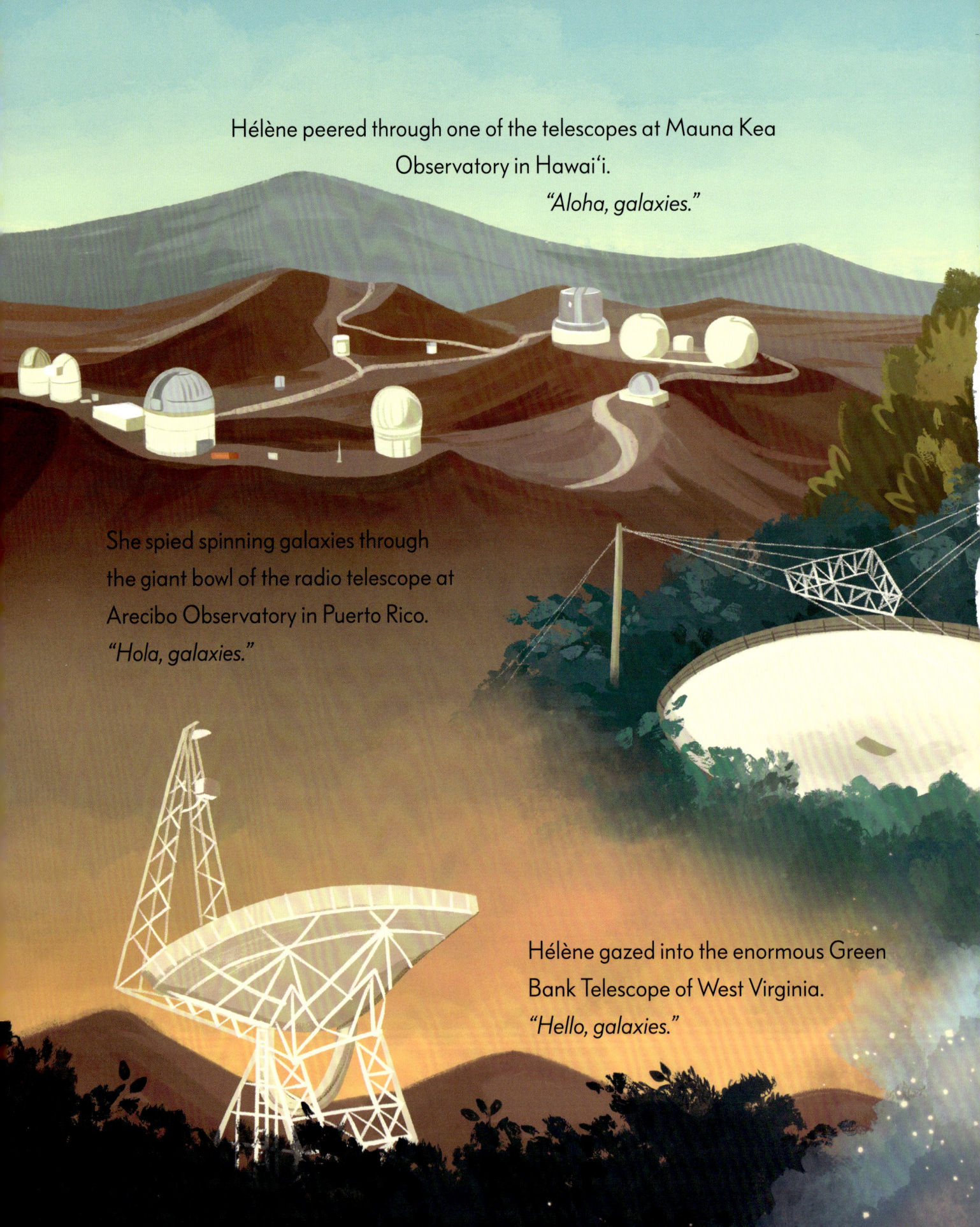

Hélène peered through one of the telescopes at Mauna Kea Observatory in Hawai'i.
"Aloha, galaxies."

She spied spinning galaxies through the giant bowl of the radio telescope at Arecibo Observatory in Puerto Rico.
"Hola, galaxies."

Hélène gazed into the enormous Green Bank Telescope of West Virginia.
"Hello, galaxies."

She measured many galaxies from the telescope at the Nançay Radio Observatory in France.
"Bonjour, galaxies."

Hélène and her team of cosmologists around the world were able to observe the night sky in three time zones at once, equaling 480 total nights of observation in one year. Sometimes, it felt like her head was spinning faster than the galaxies she gazed at.

Looking at the map they had made, Hélène and her team started to notice something really,

really,

really

big.

"It's a giant continent of more than one hundred thousand large galaxies!" Hélène and her team announced.

"The galaxies are flowing, like water down a mountain," Hélène said, thinking back to the water rolling down the steep slopes of the Alps in her small French village. "Thousands of galaxies are moving like a waterfall, and our Milky Way galaxy is a part of it!"

It was indeed a giant gathering of galaxies—a **supercluster**. It has more than 100 quadrillion suns, and it would take 500 million years to travel at the **speed of light** from one side to the other.

Hélène and her team gave the newly discovered supercluster the name Laniakea, which means "immense heaven" in Hawaiian. This name honors the ancient Polynesian navigators who used the stars and ocean **swells** as maps to find their way in waters long ago.

With the discovery of Laniakea, Hélène and her team have mapped our greater cosmic neighborhood. We live on planet Earth, revolving around the Sun in our solar system, nestled in one of the spiral arms of the Milky Way galaxy, which we now know is part of the Laniakea supercluster of galaxies.

Hélène took out her binoculars to say hello again to her faithful friend. *What is beyond the moon?* Hélène now had the answer to that question.

While people discuss her findings,

Hélène observes.

Hélène questions.

Hélène has Ideas.

And the moon is always waiting for her. *And it is waiting for you, too!*

TIME LINE

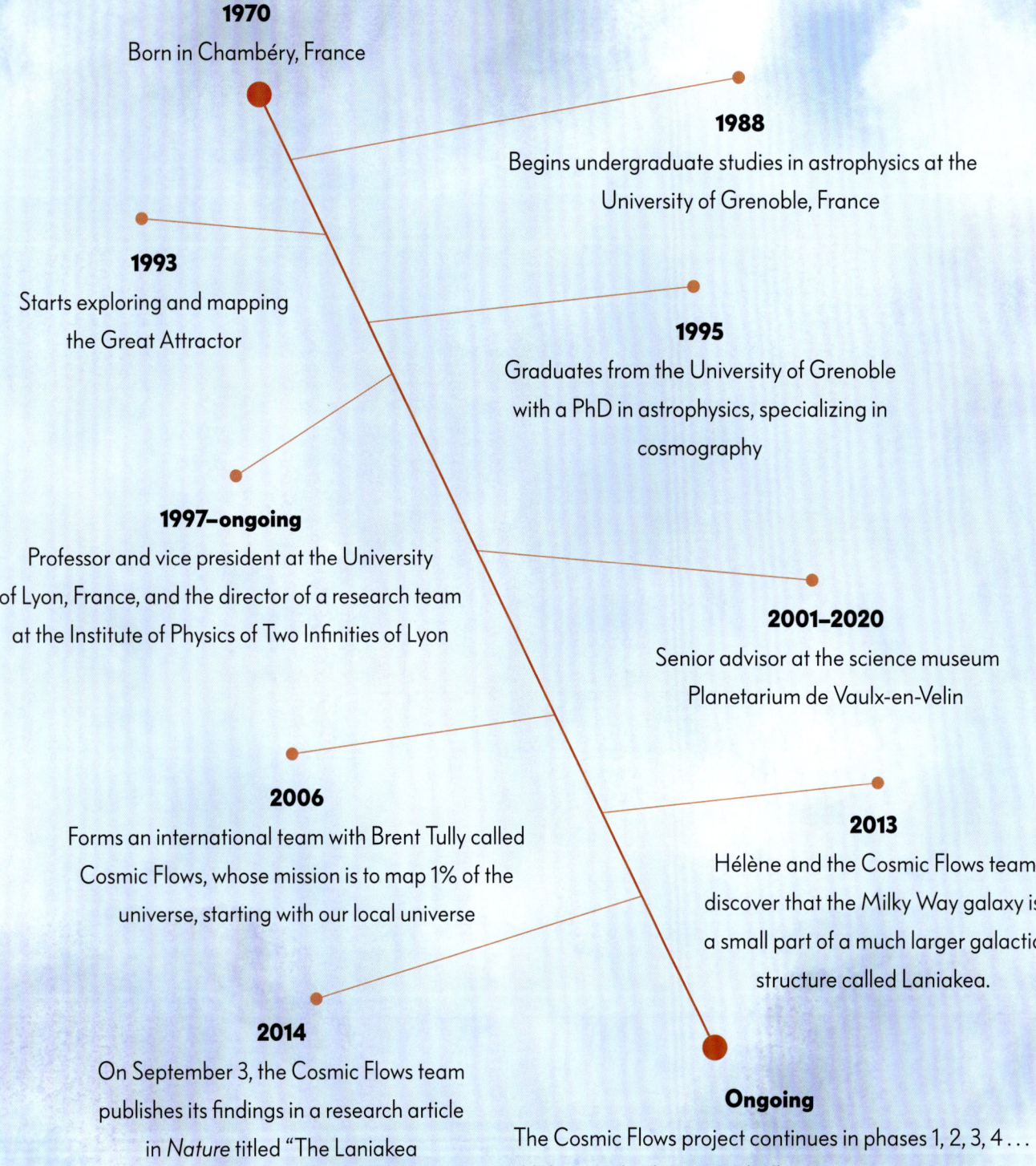

1970
Born in Chambéry, France

1988
Begins undergraduate studies in astrophysics at the University of Grenoble, France

1993
Starts exploring and mapping the Great Attractor

1995
Graduates from the University of Grenoble with a PhD in astrophysics, specializing in cosmography

1997–ongoing
Professor and vice president at the University of Lyon, France, and the director of a research team at the Institute of Physics of Two Infinities of Lyon

2001–2020
Senior advisor at the science museum Planetarium de Vaulx-en-Velin

2006
Forms an international team with Brent Tully called Cosmic Flows, whose mission is to map 1% of the universe, starting with our local universe

2013
Hélène and the Cosmic Flows team discover that the Milky Way galaxy is a small part of a much larger galactic structure called Laniakea.

2014
On September 3, the Cosmic Flows team publishes its findings in a research article in *Nature* titled "The Laniakea Supercluster of Galaxies."

Ongoing
The Cosmic Flows project continues in phases 1, 2, 3, 4 . . . Hélène embarks on goodwill tours to encourage young people (especially girls) to pursue their dreams in science.

GLOSSARY OF GALACTIC TERMS

astronomy: the scientific study of space through the observation of planets, stars, and other natural objects

astrophysics: the scientific field that uses physics and other theories to explain what is happening in the universe, including stars, planets, galaxies, and other natural objects in space

cosmographer: a scientist that maps space landscapes

cosmology: a large branch of astronomy that studies how the universe evolved. People in this profession also study the current universe and its structures and determine how they interact with one another.

dark matter: massive particles that emit no light and are invisible to us. Dr. Chanda Prescod-Weinstein suggests it should be more accurately named "invisible matter." Scientists still don't know what dark matter is, but they know it makes up most of the matter in space and think it is responsible for keeping our galaxies together.

dynamic map: a map that shows the location of an object, like a galaxy, and its movement over time

galaxy: a grouping of stars in the universe

Great Attractor: a large amount of mass (probably made of both dark matter and galaxies) that appears to be drawing local galaxies toward it

luminosity: how bright something is. Luminosity is often used to determine the distance and size of an object, like a star.

luminosity method: a mathematical formula that can be used to determine an object's distance from Earth. It is useful to cosmographers when mapping space structures like galaxies.

observatory: a location used to observe the natural world. An astronomical observatory typically houses a professional telescope used for observing outer space.

physics: the scientific study of energy and matter and how they interact with each other

plasma: electrified gas, also known as the fourth state of matter (in addition to solid, liquid, and gas). Ninety-nine percent of our visible universe is plasma, including the sun, neon signs, auroras, fire, and lightning.

plasma physics: the scientific study of plasma as matter and how it interacts with other matter and energy in space and time

speed of light: the speed at which light travels, approximately 300,000 kilometers per second, or 186,282 miles per second

supercluster: an enormous group of hundreds of thousands of large galaxies

swell: a long series of waves created and spread by weather forces thousands of miles away, including wind that blows over the open ocean without obstacles

universe: everything that exists, has ever existed, or will ever exist

OTHER FIERCELY INTELLIGENT WOMEN IN ASTRONOMY

Sandra Faber (1944–): Faber broke ground as the first woman to be accepted on the faculty of the Lick Observatory at the University of California. Faber has since spent her entire career at the University of California, Santa Cruz. She researches the effects of dark matter on the creation of galaxies. Faber led the team of astronomers that discovered the Great Attractor.

Renée Kraan-Korteweg (1954–): Kraan-Korteweg is an astronomer who has devoted her career to exploring the Great Attractor. She also develops programs in astrophysics both at the University of Cape Town and in South African townships. In 1996, Kraan-Korteweg found evidence of the Norma Cluster, which helped progress the idea that the Great Attractor could be a massive wall of galaxies.

Henrietta Swan Leavitt (1868–1921): While recording data on stars, Leavitt discovered a relationship that made it possible to calculate a star's distance from Earth. Using Leavitt's methods, Edwin Hubble was able to figure out that the universe is much bigger than our Milky Way. Leavitt's work also enabled researchers to measure the distance of galaxies beyond the Milky Way for the first time.

Chanda Prescod-Weinstein (1982–): Prescod-Weinstein was the fifty-fourth Black American woman to receive a doctorate in physics and is often the only Black physicist in any room. Prescod-Weinstein is an assistant professor of physics at the University of New Hampshire, where she researches dark matter, cosmology, and neutron stars as well as Black feminist science. She also works tirelessly to improve conditions for underrepresented and marginalized people in science.

Vera Rubin (1928–2016): In 1965, Rubin was the first woman allowed to use a telescope at the Palomar Observatory in California. During her studies, she was denied the opportunity to earn a master's degree at Princeton because she was a woman, so she went to Cornell University instead. She went on to get a PhD from Georgetown University. In 1980, Rubin published a paper that suggested the presence of dark matter in the universe, an observation that has now been confirmed and accepted by scientists across the globe.

WHERE IS A GOOD LOCATION TO BUILD A PROFESSIONAL TELESCOPE?

DARK and QUIET: A telescope should be far from human habitation. Humans, particularly in our cities and towns, create an abundance of light, particles, and radio noise that make it harder to see the night sky.

DRY: It's best to find a dry location because moisture makes night-sky images appear blurry.

HIGH: The higher a place is, the thinner the atmosphere. A thinner atmosphere makes it easier to get clear images.

SELECTED BIBLIOGRAPHY

Courtois, Hélène. Email interview with Allie Summers. March 4, 2021.

Courtois, Hélène. *Finding Our Place in the Universe: How We Discovered Laniakea, the Milky Way's Home*. Cambridge, MA: MIT Press, 2019.

Faber, Sandra. Curriculum Vitae. http://www.ucolick.org/~faber/faber_cv_09-06.pdf. Accessed March 27, 2021.

Mooney, Carla. *Telescopes*. Vero Beach, FL: Rourke, 2018.

Prescod-Weinstein, Chanda. *The Disordered Cosmos: A Journey into Dark Matter, Spacetime, and Dreams Deferred*. New York: Bold Type Books, 2021.

Sparrow, Giles. *Universe*. DKfindout! New York: Dorling Kindersley, 2018.

Stoddart, Charlotte, ed. "Laniakea: Our Home Supercluster." September 4, 2014. *Nature* video, 4:10. https://www.youtube.com/watch?v=rENyyRwxpHo.

Vives, François-Xavier, dir. *Cosmic Flows: The Cartographers of the Universe*. Camera Lucida Productions, 2019.

ACKNOWLEDGMENTS

Thank you, Hélène Courtois, for your participation and support during the writing of this book. I'm so grateful for all the time you spent answering my questions and patiently explaining the complexities of astrophysics to me. I am over the moon that kids around the world will get to learn about you and your phenomenal discovery.

I also want to acknowledge and honor the Indigenous peoples across the world whose sacred lands have been used to build telescopes for the progression of science.

Lastly, thank you, Jenna Ishii Menen, crew member of the Polynesian Voyaging Society, for your assistance with cultural accuracy.

✳

ALLIE SUMMERS is a nonfiction children's book author. Her favorite things to write about are nature and incredible women in science. She is fascinated by the fact that most of the elements in our human bodies were formed in stars billions of years ago. When she is not writing, she can most likely be found outside: running, surfing, foraging, climbing, roller-skating, or stargazing. Allie Summers lives with her family in the Laniakea supercluster, on a small blue planet called Earth, in a town known as San Francisco.

SIAN JAMES is an early medieval archaeologist and the illustrator of many books, including the Escape Room Adventures series by Alex Woolf and *Dream Big for Kids* by Bob Goff and Lindsey Goff Viducich. Born and raised in Hong Kong, she has been drawing ever since she was able to pick up a pen. When she is not creating art, she loves reading fantasy novels, baking cakes, gardening, and drinking too much tea. Sian James lives in Cambridge, England, with her husband, their daughter, and two affectionate cats.

"Just follow your heart and do what you like." —Hélène Courtois

✳

For my sunshine, my little star, and my moon—I love you to the stars and back!
AS

To Mum, who inspired me to reach for the skies, and to Rosie, for whom I hope to do the same
SJ

The MIT Press, the ☰mit Kids Press colophon, and MIT Kids Press are trademarks of The MIT Press,
a department of the Massachusetts Institute of Technology, and used under license from The MIT Press.
The colophon and MIT Kids Press are registered in the US Patent and Trademark Office.

First edition 2025

Library of Congress Catalog Card Number pending
ISBN 978-1-5362-2897-7

25 26 27 28 29 30 CCP 10 9 8 7 6 5 4 3 2 1

Printed in Shenzhen, Guangdong, China

This book was typeset in Bauer Grotesk OT.
The illustrations were created digitally.

MIT Kids Press
an imprint of Candlewick Press
99 Dover Street
Somerville, Massachusetts 02144

mitkidspress.com
candlewick.com

EU Authorized Representative: HackettFlynn Ltd., 36 Cloch Choirneal,
Balrothery, Co. Dublin, K32 C942, Ireland. EU@walkerpublishinggroup.com